Sprinting Training Log and Diary

This Book Belongs To:

_____

Visit http://elegantnotebooks.com for more
sports training books.

Training Log and Diary
Nutrition Log and Diary
Strength and Conditioning Log and Diary

DATE:		WEEK:		HOURS TRAINED:	
COACH:				TIME:	

GOALS

WARM UP/ DRILLS

TECHNIQUE 1

TECHNIQUE 2

NOTES

DATE: **WEEK:** **HOURS TRAINED:**

COACH: **TIME:**

GOALS

WARM UP/ DRILLS

TECHNIQUE 1

TECHNIQUE 2

NOTES

DATE:		WEEK:		HOURS TRAINED:	
COACH:				TIME:	

GOALS

WARM UP/ DRILLS

TECHNIQUE 1

TECHNIQUE 2

NOTES

DATE: _____   **WEEK:** _____   **HOURS TRAINED:** _____

COACH: _____   **TIME:** _____

GOALS

WARM UP/ DRILLS

TECHNIQUE 1

TECHNIQUE 2

NOTES

DATE: _____ **WEEK:** _____ **HOURS TRAINED:** _____

COACH: _____ **TIME:** _____

GOALS

WARM UP/ DRILLS

TECHNIQUE 1

TECHNIQUE 2

NOTES

DATE: **WEEK:**   **HOURS TRAINED:**

COACH: **TIME:**

GOALS

WARM UP/ DRILLS

TECHNIQUE 1

TECHNIQUE 2

NOTES

DATE:		WEEK:		HOURS TRAINED:	

COACH:		TIME:	

GOALS

WARM UP/ DRILLS

TECHNIQUE 1

TECHNIQUE 2

NOTES

DATE: _____ **WEEK:** _____ **HOURS TRAINED:** _____

COACH: _____ **TIME:** _____

GOALS

WARM UP/ DRILLS

TECHNIQUE 1

TECHNIQUE 2

NOTES

DATE: _____ **WEEK:** _____ **HOURS TRAINED:** _____

COACH: _____ **TIME:** _____

GOALS

WARM UP/ DRILLS

TECHNIQUE 1

TECHNIQUE 2

NOTES

DATE: _____ **WEEK:** _____ **HOURS TRAINED:** _____

COACH: _____ **TIME:** _____

GOALS

WARM UP/ DRILLS

TECHNIQUE 1

TECHNIQUE 2

NOTES

DATE: _____ **WEEK:** _____ **HOURS TRAINED:** _____

COACH: _____ **TIME:** _____

GOALS

WARM UP/ DRILLS

TECHNIQUE 1

TECHNIQUE 2

NOTES

DATE: _____ **WEEK:** _____ **HOURS TRAINED:** _____

COACH: _____ **TIME:** _____

GOALS

WARM UP/ DRILLS

TECHNIQUE 1

TECHNIQUE 2

NOTES

DATE:		WEEK:		HOURS TRAINED:	
COACH:				TIME:	

GOALS

WARM UP/ DRILLS

TECHNIQUE 1

TECHNIQUE 2

NOTES

DATE: [ ] **WEEK:** [ ] **HOURS TRAINED:** [ ]

COACH: [ ] **TIME:** [ ]

GOALS

WARM UP/ DRILLS

TECHNIQUE 1

TECHNIQUE 2

NOTES

DATE: _____   **WEEK:** _____   **HOURS TRAINED:** _____

COACH: _____   **TIME:** _____

GOALS

WARM UP/ DRILLS

TECHNIQUE 1

TECHNIQUE 2

NOTES

DATE: _____ **WEEK:** _____ **HOURS TRAINED:** _____

COACH: _____ **TIME:** _____

GOALS

WARM UP/ DRILLS

TECHNIQUE 1

TECHNIQUE 2

NOTES

DATE: **WEEK:**   **HOURS TRAINED:**

COACH: **TIME:**

GOALS

WARM UP/ DRILLS

TECHNIQUE 1

TECHNIQUE 2

NOTES

DATE: _____   **WEEK:** _____   **HOURS TRAINED:** _____

COACH: _____   **TIME:** _____

GOALS

WARM UP/ DRILLS

TECHNIQUE 1

TECHNIQUE 2

NOTES

DATE: _____ **WEEK:** _____ **HOURS TRAINED:** _____

COACH: _____ **TIME:** _____

GOALS

WARM UP/ DRILLS

TECHNIQUE 1

TECHNIQUE 2

NOTES

DATE: **WEEK:**   **HOURS TRAINED:**

COACH: **TIME:**

GOALS

WARM UP/ DRILLS

TECHNIQUE 1

TECHNIQUE 2

NOTES

DATE: _____ **WEEK:** _____ **HOURS TRAINED:** _____

COACH: _____ **TIME:** _____

GOALS

WARM UP/ DRILLS

TECHNIQUE 1

TECHNIQUE 2

NOTES

DATE: **WEEK:** **HOURS TRAINED:**

COACH: **TIME:**

GOALS

WARM UP/ DRILLS

TECHNIQUE 1

TECHNIQUE 2

NOTES

DATE: **WEEK:**   **HOURS TRAINED:**

COACH: **TIME:**

GOALS

WARM UP/ DRILLS

TECHNIQUE 1

TECHNIQUE 2

NOTES

DATE: _____ **WEEK:** _____ **HOURS TRAINED:** _____

COACH: _____ **TIME:** _____

GOALS

WARM UP/ DRILLS

TECHNIQUE 1

TECHNIQUE 2

NOTES

DATE:		WEEK:		HOURS TRAINED:	

COACH:			TIME:	

GOALS

WARM UP/ DRILLS

TECHNIQUE 1

TECHNIQUE 2

NOTES

DATE: [   ] **WEEK:** [   ] **HOURS TRAINED:** [   ]

COACH: [   ] **TIME:** [   ]

GOALS

WARM UP/ DRILLS

TECHNIQUE 1

TECHNIQUE 2

NOTES

DATE: **WEEK:**   **HOURS TRAINED:**

COACH: **TIME:**

GOALS

WARM UP/ DRILLS

TECHNIQUE 1

TECHNIQUE 2

NOTES

DATE: _____ **WEEK:** _____ **HOURS TRAINED:** _____

COACH: _____ **TIME:** _____

GOALS

WARM UP/ DRILLS

TECHNIQUE 1

TECHNIQUE 2

NOTES

DATE: _____ **WEEK:** _____ **HOURS TRAINED:** _____

COACH: _____ **TIME:** _____

GOALS

WARM UP/ DRILLS

TECHNIQUE 1

TECHNIQUE 2

NOTES

DATE: _____ **WEEK:** _____ **HOURS TRAINED:** _____

COACH: _____ **TIME:** _____

GOALS

WARM UP/ DRILLS

TECHNIQUE 1

TECHNIQUE 2

NOTES

DATE: _____ **WEEK:** _____ **HOURS TRAINED:** _____

COACH: _____ **TIME:** _____

GOALS

WARM UP/ DRILLS

TECHNIQUE 1

TECHNIQUE 2

NOTES

DATE: [ ]   **WEEK:** [ ]   **HOURS TRAINED:** [ ]

COACH: [ ]   **TIME:** [ ]

GOALS

WARM UP/ DRILLS

TECHNIQUE 1

TECHNIQUE 2

NOTES

DATE: **WEEK:**   **HOURS TRAINED:**

COACH: **TIME:**

GOALS

WARM UP/ DRILLS

TECHNIQUE 1

TECHNIQUE 2

NOTES

DATE: **WEEK:** **HOURS TRAINED:**

COACH: **TIME:**

GOALS

WARM UP/ DRILLS

TECHNIQUE 1

TECHNIQUE 2

NOTES

DATE: [ ] **WEEK:** [ ] **HOURS TRAINED:** [ ]

COACH: [ ] **TIME:** [ ]

GOALS

WARM UP/ DRILLS

TECHNIQUE 1

TECHNIQUE 2

NOTES

DATE: _____ **WEEK:** _____ **HOURS TRAINED:** _____

COACH: _____ **TIME:** _____

GOALS

WARM UP/ DRILLS

TECHNIQUE 1

TECHNIQUE 2

NOTES

DATE: **WEEK:**   **HOURS TRAINED:**

COACH: **TIME:**

GOALS

WARM UP/ DRILLS

TECHNIQUE 1

TECHNIQUE 2

NOTES

DATE: _____   **WEEK:** _____   **HOURS TRAINED:** _____

COACH: _____   **TIME:** _____

GOALS

WARM UP/ DRILLS

TECHNIQUE 1

TECHNIQUE 2

NOTES

DATE: [ ] **WEEK:** [ ] **HOURS TRAINED:** [ ]

COACH: [ ] **TIME:** [ ]

GOALS

WARM UP/ DRILLS

TECHNIQUE 1

TECHNIQUE 2

NOTES

DATE: _____ **WEEK:** _____ **HOURS TRAINED:** _____

COACH: _____ **TIME:** _____

GOALS

WARM UP/ DRILLS

TECHNIQUE 1

TECHNIQUE 2

NOTES

DATE: **WEEK:**   **HOURS TRAINED:**

COACH: **TIME:**

GOALS

WARM UP/ DRILLS

TECHNIQUE 1

TECHNIQUE 2

NOTES

DATE: [   ] **WEEK:** [   ] **HOURS TRAINED:** [   ]

COACH: [   ] **TIME:** [   ]

GOALS

WARM UP/ DRILLS

TECHNIQUE 1

TECHNIQUE 2

NOTES

DATE: _____ **WEEK:** _____ **HOURS TRAINED:** _____

COACH: _____ **TIME:** _____

GOALS

WARM UP/ DRILLS

TECHNIQUE 1

TECHNIQUE 2

NOTES

DATE: _____ **WEEK:** _____ **HOURS TRAINED:** _____

COACH: _____ **TIME:** _____

GOALS

WARM UP/ DRILLS

TECHNIQUE 1

TECHNIQUE 2

NOTES

DATE: **WEEK:**   **HOURS TRAINED:**

COACH: **TIME:**

GOALS

WARM UP/ DRILLS

TECHNIQUE 1

TECHNIQUE 2

NOTES

DATE: **WEEK:** **HOURS TRAINED:**

COACH: **TIME:**

GOALS

WARM UP/ DRILLS

TECHNIQUE 1

TECHNIQUE 2

NOTES

DATE: **WEEK:**   **HOURS TRAINED:**

COACH: **TIME:**

GOALS

WARM UP/ DRILLS

TECHNIQUE 1

TECHNIQUE 2

NOTES

DATE: _____ **WEEK:** _____ **HOURS TRAINED:** _____

COACH: _____ **TIME:** _____

GOALS

WARM UP/ DRILLS

TECHNIQUE 1

TECHNIQUE 2

NOTES

DATE: [   ] **WEEK:** [   ] **HOURS TRAINED:** [   ]

COACH: [   ] **TIME:** [   ]

GOALS

WARM UP/ DRILLS

TECHNIQUE 1

TECHNIQUE 2

NOTES

DATE: _____ **WEEK:** _____ **HOURS TRAINED:** _____

COACH: _____ **TIME:** _____

GOALS

WARM UP/ DRILLS

TECHNIQUE 1

TECHNIQUE 2

NOTES

DATE: _____ **WEEK:** _____ **HOURS TRAINED:** _____

COACH: _____ **TIME:** _____

GOALS

WARM UP/ DRILLS

TECHNIQUE 1

TECHNIQUE 2

NOTES

DATE: _____ **WEEK:** _____ **HOURS TRAINED:** _____

COACH: _____ **TIME:** _____

GOALS

WARM UP/ DRILLS

TECHNIQUE 1

TECHNIQUE 2

NOTES

DATE: _____ **WEEK:** _____ **HOURS TRAINED:** _____

COACH: _____ **TIME:** _____

GOALS

WARM UP/ DRILLS

TECHNIQUE 1

TECHNIQUE 2

NOTES

DATE: [　　　　　] **WEEK:** [　　] **HOURS TRAINED:** [　　　　]

COACH: [　　　　　　　　] **TIME:** [　　　]

GOALS

WARM UP/ DRILLS

TECHNIQUE 1

TECHNIQUE 2

NOTES

DATE: [ ] **WEEK:** [ ] **HOURS TRAINED:** [ ]

COACH: [ ] **TIME:** [ ]

GOALS

WARM UP/ DRILLS

TECHNIQUE 1

TECHNIQUE 2

NOTES

DATE: **WEEK:** **HOURS TRAINED:**

COACH: **TIME:**

GOALS

WARM UP/ DRILLS

TECHNIQUE 1

TECHNIQUE 2

NOTES

DATE: _____ **WEEK:** _____ **HOURS TRAINED:** _____

COACH: _____ **TIME:** _____

GOALS

WARM UP/ DRILLS

TECHNIQUE 1

TECHNIQUE 2

NOTES

DATE: **WEEK:** **HOURS TRAINED:**

COACH: **TIME:**

GOALS

WARM UP/ DRILLS

TECHNIQUE 1

TECHNIQUE 2

NOTES

DATE: [ ] **WEEK:** [ ] **HOURS TRAINED:** [ ]

COACH: [ ] **TIME:** [ ]

GOALS

WARM UP/ DRILLS

TECHNIQUE 1

TECHNIQUE 2

NOTES

DATE: | **WEEK:** | **HOURS TRAINED:**

COACH: | **TIME:**

GOALS

WARM UP/ DRILLS

TECHNIQUE 1

TECHNIQUE 2

NOTES

DATE: _____ **WEEK:** _____ **HOURS TRAINED:** _____

COACH: _____ **TIME:** _____

GOALS

WARM UP/ DRILLS

TECHNIQUE 1

TECHNIQUE 2

NOTES

DATE: **WEEK:** **HOURS TRAINED:**

COACH: **TIME:**

GOALS

WARM UP/ DRILLS

TECHNIQUE 1

TECHNIQUE 2

NOTES

DATE: **WEEK:** **HOURS TRAINED:**

COACH: **TIME:**

GOALS

WARM UP/ DRILLS

TECHNIQUE 1

TECHNIQUE 2

NOTES

DATE: _____   **WEEK:** _____   **HOURS TRAINED:** _____

COACH: _____   **TIME:** _____

GOALS

WARM UP/ DRILLS

TECHNIQUE 1

TECHNIQUE 2

NOTES

DATE: _____ **WEEK:** _____ **HOURS TRAINED:** _____

COACH: _____ **TIME:** _____

GOALS

WARM UP/ DRILLS

TECHNIQUE 1

TECHNIQUE 2

NOTES

DATE: [   ]   **WEEK:** [   ]   **HOURS TRAINED:** [   ]

COACH: [   ]   **TIME:** [   ]

GOALS

WARM UP/ DRILLS

TECHNIQUE 1

TECHNIQUE 2

NOTES

DATE: _____ **WEEK:** _____ **HOURS TRAINED:** _____

COACH: _____ **TIME:** _____

GOALS

WARM UP/ DRILLS

TECHNIQUE 1

TECHNIQUE 2

NOTES

DATE: _____ **WEEK:** _____ **HOURS TRAINED:** _____

COACH: _____ **TIME:** _____

GOALS

WARM UP/ DRILLS

TECHNIQUE 1

TECHNIQUE 2

NOTES

DATE: | **WEEK:** | **HOURS TRAINED:**

COACH: | **TIME:**

GOALS

WARM UP/ DRILLS

TECHNIQUE 1

TECHNIQUE 2

NOTES

DATE: _____ **WEEK:** _____ **HOURS TRAINED:** _____

COACH: _____ **TIME:** _____

GOALS

WARM UP/ DRILLS

TECHNIQUE 1

TECHNIQUE 2

NOTES

DATE: [   ] **WEEK:** [   ] **HOURS TRAINED:** [   ]

COACH: [   ] **TIME:** [   ]

GOALS

WARM UP/ DRILLS

TECHNIQUE 1

TECHNIQUE 2

NOTES

DATE: _____ **WEEK:** _____ **HOURS TRAINED:** _____

COACH: _____ **TIME:** _____

GOALS

WARM UP/ DRILLS

TECHNIQUE 1

TECHNIQUE 2

NOTES

DATE: [   ]   **WEEK:** [   ]   **HOURS TRAINED:** [   ]

COACH: [   ]   **TIME:** [   ]

GOALS

WARM UP/ DRILLS

TECHNIQUE 1

TECHNIQUE 2

NOTES

DATE: _____ **WEEK:** _____ **HOURS TRAINED:** _____

COACH: _____ **TIME:** _____

GOALS

WARM UP/ DRILLS

TECHNIQUE 1

TECHNIQUE 2

NOTES

DATE: [   ] **WEEK:** [   ] **HOURS TRAINED:** [   ]

COACH: [   ] **TIME:** [   ]

GOALS

WARM UP/ DRILLS

TECHNIQUE 1

TECHNIQUE 2

NOTES

DATE: _____ **WEEK:** _____ **HOURS TRAINED:** _____

COACH: _____ **TIME:** _____

GOALS

WARM UP/ DRILLS

TECHNIQUE 1

TECHNIQUE 2

NOTES

DATE:		WEEK:		HOURS TRAINED:	

COACH:		TIME:	

GOALS

WARM UP/ DRILLS

TECHNIQUE 1

TECHNIQUE 2

NOTES

DATE: _____ **WEEK:** ___ **HOURS TRAINED:** _____

COACH: _____ **TIME:** _____

GOALS

WARM UP/ DRILLS

TECHNIQUE 1

TECHNIQUE 2

NOTES

DATE:		WEEK:		HOURS TRAINED:	
COACH:				TIME:	

GOALS

WARM UP/ DRILLS

TECHNIQUE 1

TECHNIQUE 2

NOTES

DATE: [ ] **WEEK:** [ ] **HOURS TRAINED:** [ ]

COACH: [ ] **TIME:** [ ]

GOALS

WARM UP/ DRILLS

TECHNIQUE 1

TECHNIQUE 2

NOTES

DATE: _____ **WEEK:** _____ **HOURS TRAINED:** _____

COACH: _____ **TIME:** _____

GOALS

WARM UP/ DRILLS

TECHNIQUE 1

TECHNIQUE 2

NOTES

DATE: _____ **WEEK:** _____ **HOURS TRAINED:** _____

COACH: _____ **TIME:** _____

GOALS

WARM UP/ DRILLS

TECHNIQUE 1

TECHNIQUE 2

NOTES

DATE: _____ **WEEK:** _____ **HOURS TRAINED:** _____

COACH: _____ **TIME:** _____

GOALS

WARM UP/ DRILLS

TECHNIQUE 1

TECHNIQUE 2

NOTES

DATE: [   ] **WEEK:** [   ] **HOURS TRAINED:** [   ]

COACH: [   ] **TIME:** [   ]

GOALS

WARM UP/ DRILLS

TECHNIQUE 1

TECHNIQUE 2

NOTES

DATE: **WEEK:**   **HOURS TRAINED:**

COACH: **TIME:**

GOALS

WARM UP/ DRILLS

TECHNIQUE 1

TECHNIQUE 2

NOTES

DATE: _____ **WEEK:** _____ **HOURS TRAINED:** _____

COACH: _____ **TIME:** _____

GOALS

WARM UP/ DRILLS

TECHNIQUE 1

TECHNIQUE 2

NOTES

DATE: **WEEK:**   **HOURS TRAINED:**

COACH: **TIME:**

GOALS

WARM UP/ DRILLS

TECHNIQUE 1

TECHNIQUE 2

NOTES

DATE: [ ] **WEEK:** [ ] **HOURS TRAINED:** [ ]

COACH: [ ] **TIME:** [ ]

GOALS

WARM UP/ DRILLS

TECHNIQUE 1

TECHNIQUE 2

NOTES

DATE: _____ **WEEK:** _____ **HOURS TRAINED:** _____

COACH: _____ **TIME:** _____

GOALS

WARM UP/ DRILLS

TECHNIQUE 1

TECHNIQUE 2

NOTES

DATE: _____ **WEEK:** _____ **HOURS TRAINED:** _____

COACH: _____ **TIME:** _____

GOALS

WARM UP/ DRILLS

TECHNIQUE 1

TECHNIQUE 2

NOTES

DATE: _____ **WEEK:** _____ **HOURS TRAINED:** _____

COACH: _____ **TIME:** _____

GOALS

WARM UP/ DRILLS

TECHNIQUE 1

TECHNIQUE 2

NOTES

DATE: [   ]   **WEEK:** [   ]   **HOURS TRAINED:** [   ]

COACH: [   ]   **TIME:** [   ]

GOALS

WARM UP/ DRILLS

TECHNIQUE 1

TECHNIQUE 2

NOTES

DATE: _____   **WEEK:** _____   **HOURS TRAINED:** _____

COACH: _____   **TIME:** _____

GOALS

WARM UP/ DRILLS

TECHNIQUE 1

TECHNIQUE 2

NOTES

DATE: _____ **WEEK:** _____ **HOURS TRAINED:** _____

COACH: _____ **TIME:** _____

GOALS

WARM UP/ DRILLS

TECHNIQUE 1

TECHNIQUE 2

NOTES

DATE: [   ] **WEEK:** [   ] **HOURS TRAINED:** [   ]

COACH: [   ] **TIME:** [   ]

GOALS

WARM UP/ DRILLS

TECHNIQUE 1

TECHNIQUE 2

NOTES

DATE: **WEEK:**   **HOURS TRAINED:**

COACH: **TIME:**

GOALS

WARM UP/ DRILLS

TECHNIQUE 1

TECHNIQUE 2

NOTES

DATE:		WEEK:		HOURS TRAINED:	

COACH:			TIME:	

GOALS

WARM UP/ DRILLS

TECHNIQUE 1

TECHNIQUE 2

NOTES

DATE: _____ **WEEK:** _____ **HOURS TRAINED:** _____

COACH: _____ **TIME:** _____

GOALS

WARM UP/ DRILLS

TECHNIQUE 1

TECHNIQUE 2

NOTES

DATE: | **WEEK:** | **HOURS TRAINED:**

COACH: | **TIME:**

GOALS

WARM UP/ DRILLS

TECHNIQUE 1

TECHNIQUE 2

NOTES

DATE: **WEEK:**   **HOURS TRAINED:**

COACH: **TIME:**

GOALS

WARM UP/ DRILLS

TECHNIQUE 1

TECHNIQUE 2

NOTES

DATE: _____ **WEEK:** _____ **HOURS TRAINED:** _____

COACH: _____ **TIME:** _____

GOALS

WARM UP/ DRILLS

TECHNIQUE 1

TECHNIQUE 2

NOTES

DATE: **WEEK:**   **HOURS TRAINED:**

COACH: **TIME:**

GOALS

WARM UP/ DRILLS

TECHNIQUE 1

TECHNIQUE 2

NOTES

DATE: _____ **WEEK:** _____ **HOURS TRAINED:** _____

COACH: _____ **TIME:** _____

GOALS

WARM UP/ DRILLS

TECHNIQUE 1

TECHNIQUE 2

NOTES

DATE: _____ **WEEK:** _____ **HOURS TRAINED:** _____

COACH: _____ **TIME:** _____

GOALS

WARM UP/ DRILLS

TECHNIQUE 1

TECHNIQUE 2

NOTES

DATE: _____ **WEEK:** _____ **HOURS TRAINED:** _____

COACH: _____ **TIME:** _____

GOALS

WARM UP/ DRILLS

TECHNIQUE 1

TECHNIQUE 2

NOTES

DATE: _____   **WEEK:** _____   **HOURS TRAINED:** _____

COACH: _____   **TIME:** _____

GOALS

WARM UP/ DRILLS

TECHNIQUE 1

TECHNIQUE 2

NOTES

DATE: _____ **WEEK:** _____ **HOURS TRAINED:** _____

COACH: _____ **TIME:** _____

GOALS

WARM UP/ DRILLS

TECHNIQUE 1

TECHNIQUE 2

NOTES

DATE: _____ **WEEK:** _____ **HOURS TRAINED:** _____

COACH: _____ **TIME:** _____

GOALS

WARM UP/ DRILLS

TECHNIQUE 1

TECHNIQUE 2

NOTES

DATE: **WEEK:**   **HOURS TRAINED:**

COACH: **TIME:**

GOALS

WARM UP/ DRILLS

TECHNIQUE 1

TECHNIQUE 2

NOTES

DATE: [ ] **WEEK:** [ ] **HOURS TRAINED:** [ ]

COACH: [ ] **TIME:** [ ]

GOALS

WARM UP/ DRILLS

TECHNIQUE 1

TECHNIQUE 2

NOTES

DATE:		WEEK:		HOURS TRAINED:	
COACH:				TIME:	

GOALS

WARM UP/ DRILLS

TECHNIQUE 1

TECHNIQUE 2

NOTES

DATE: _____ **WEEK:** _____ **HOURS TRAINED:** _____

COACH: _____ **TIME:** _____

GOALS

WARM UP/ DRILLS

TECHNIQUE 1

TECHNIQUE 2

NOTES

DATE: _____ **WEEK:** _____ **HOURS TRAINED:** _____

COACH: _____ **TIME:** _____

GOALS

WARM UP/ DRILLS

TECHNIQUE 1

TECHNIQUE 2

NOTES

DATE: | **WEEK:** | **HOURS TRAINED:**

COACH: | **TIME:**

GOALS

WARM UP/ DRILLS

TECHNIQUE 1

TECHNIQUE 2

NOTES

DATE:		WEEK:		HOURS TRAINED:	
COACH:				TIME:	

GOALS

WARM UP/ DRILLS

TECHNIQUE 1

TECHNIQUE 2

NOTES

DATE: [ ] **WEEK:** [ ] **HOURS TRAINED:** [ ]

COACH: [ ] **TIME:** [ ]

GOALS

WARM UP/ DRILLS

TECHNIQUE 1

TECHNIQUE 2

NOTES

| DATE: | WEEK: | HOURS TRAINED: |
| COACH: | | TIME: |

GOALS

WARM UP/ DRILLS

TECHNIQUE 1

TECHNIQUE 2

NOTES

DATE: **WEEK:**   **HOURS TRAINED:**

COACH: **TIME:**

GOALS

WARM UP/ DRILLS

TECHNIQUE 1

TECHNIQUE 2

NOTES

DATE: _____ **WEEK:** _____ **HOURS TRAINED:** _____

COACH: _____ **TIME:** _____

GOALS

WARM UP/ DRILLS

TECHNIQUE 1

TECHNIQUE 2

NOTES